Baby Medical School

The Doctor's Visit

By Margot and Antonis Alesund

FROM THE CREATOR OF THE BABY BIOCHEMIST

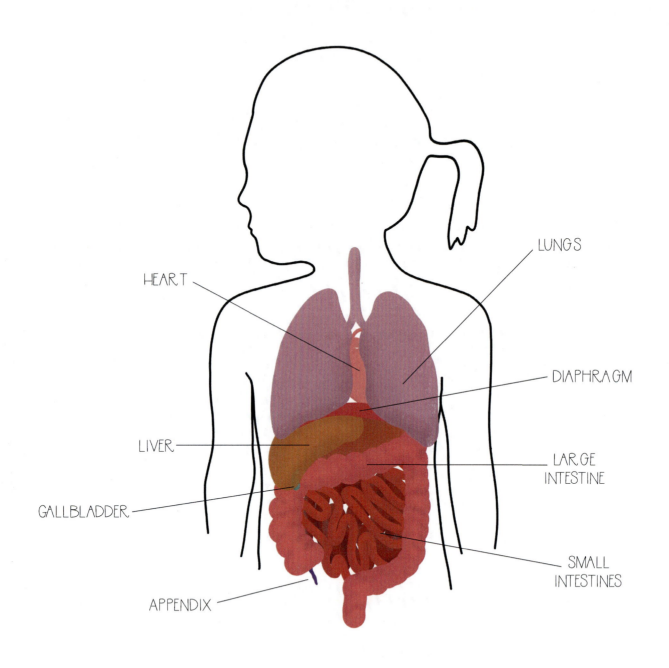

Every year, you go to the doctor's office to make sure your body is working like it should.

A nurse and doctor will check almost every part of you. They want to make sure you stay happy and healthy. Let's take a closer look at what they are checking!

The doctor will ask you and your parent questions to make sure you are getting enough sleep, exercise, and good foods.

Those are some of the most important things you can do to stay healthy!

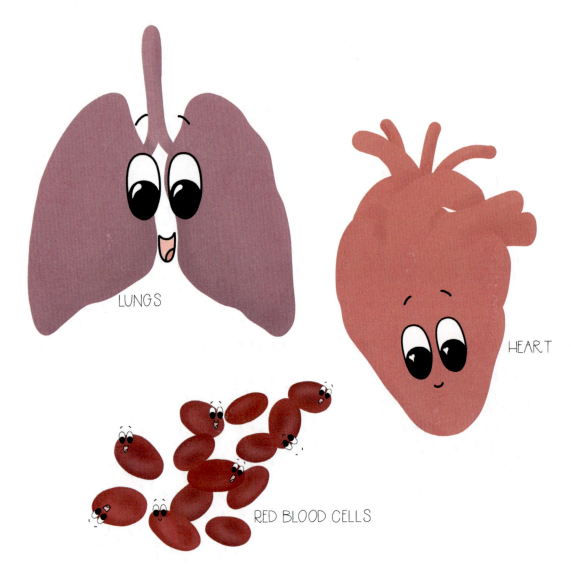

During your visit, someone will take measurements that check your blood, heart, and lungs.

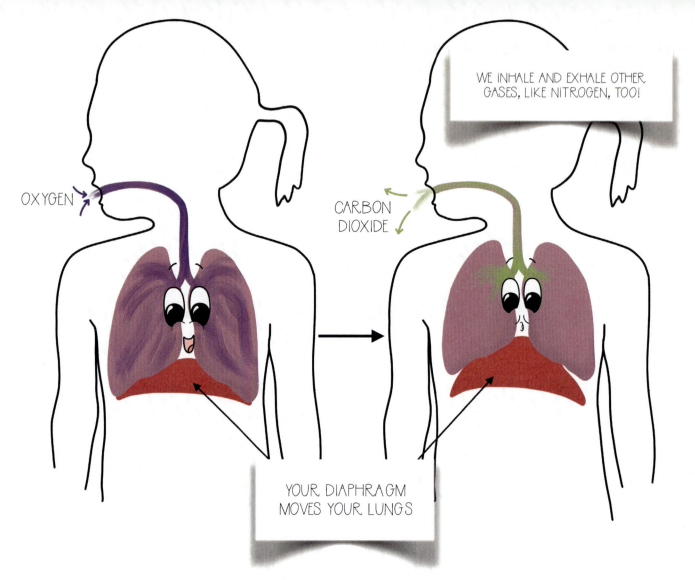

Your lungs are big ballon-like sacs in your chest that take in the air you breathe, then push out waste gases.

Your doctor will listen to your lungs with a stethoscope while you breathe.

You can actually hear the air going in and out of your lungs!

THE DOCTOR MIGHT USE A SENSOR TO MEASURE HOW MUCH OXYGEN YOUR BLOOD IS CARRYING. THIS MEASUREMENT IS CALLED OXYGEN SATURATION.

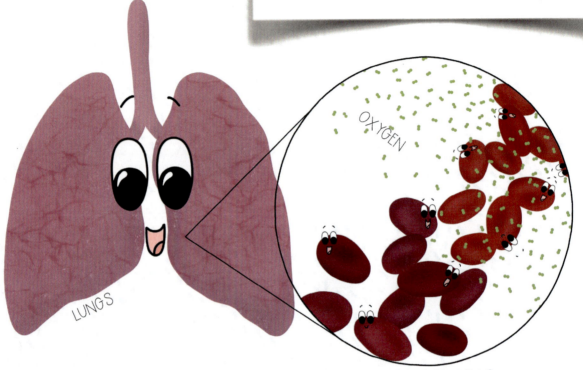

LUNGS

OXYGEN

RED BLOOD CELLS IN YOUR BLOOD

Your blood flows by your lungs, takes oxygen from them, then delivers it to your whole body.

Your body uses the oxygen to help make energy!

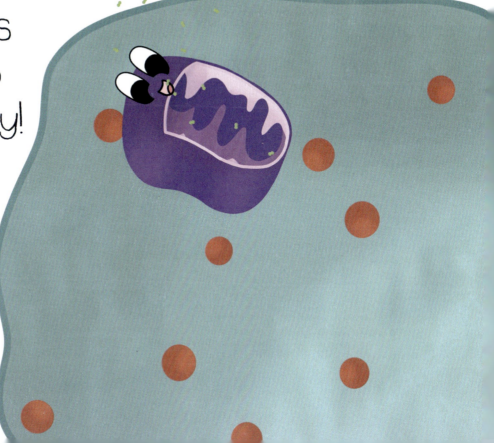

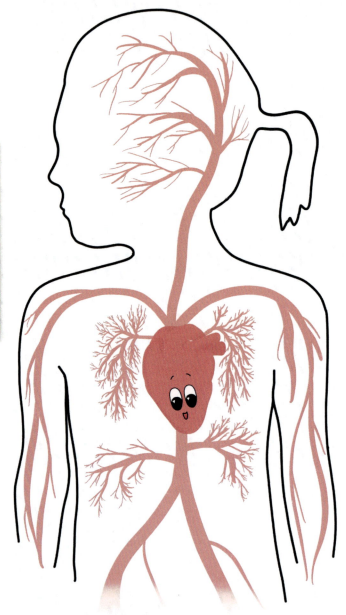

YOUR HEART IS A PUMP! WHEN YOU EXERCISE, YOUR HEART BEATS FASTER TO DELIVER MORE BLOOD TO YOUR BODY.

YOUR HEART RATE IS THE NUMBER OF TIMES YOUR HEART BEATS PER MINUTE.

Your heart is responsible for pushing that blood throughout your body.

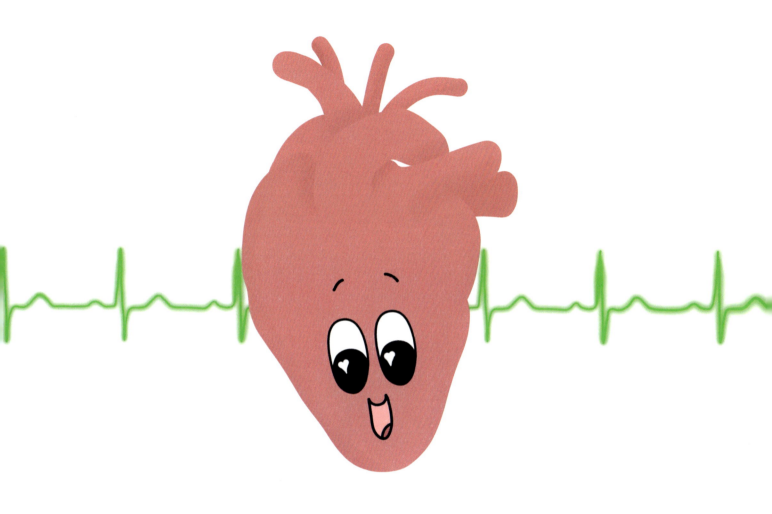

If you put your hand on your chest, you might be able to feel your heart beating!

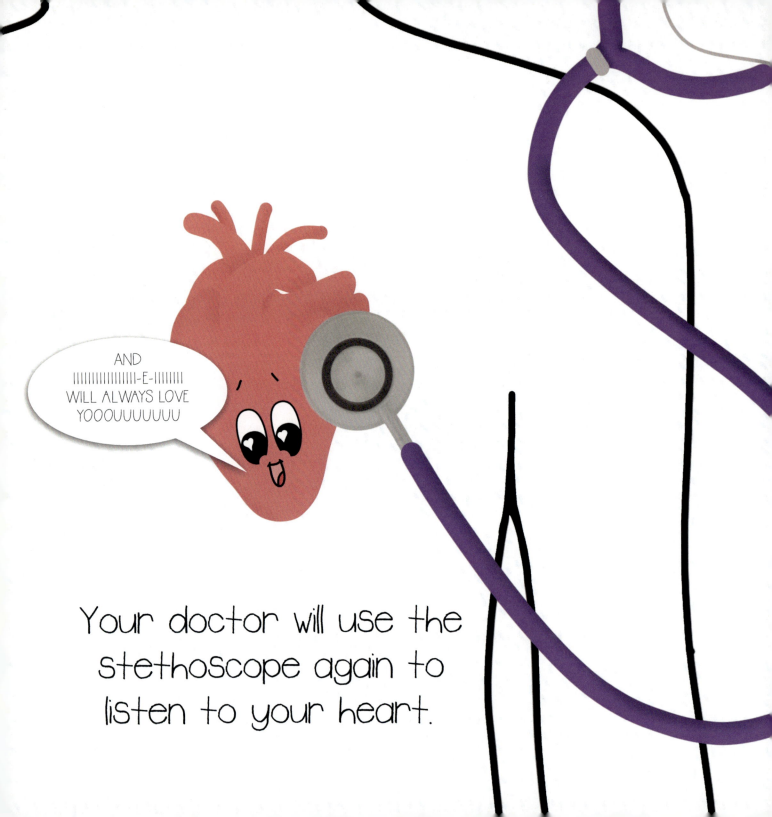

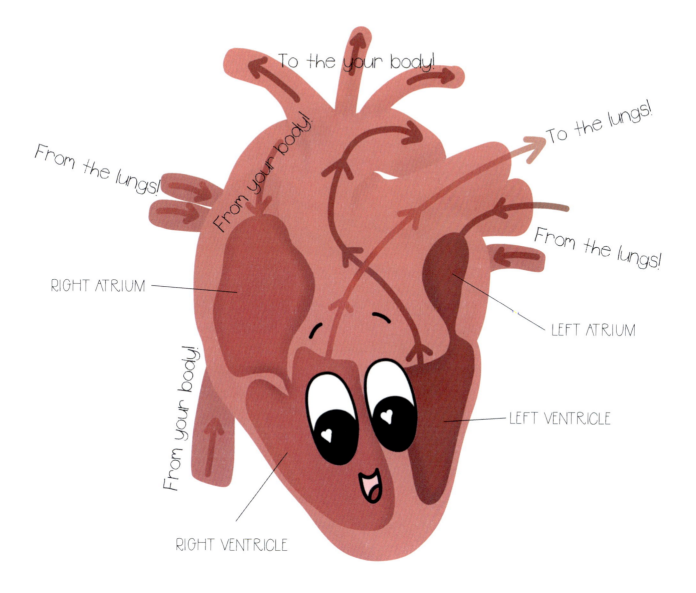

Your doctor will try to listen to the different places blood flows in your heart. The path can seem pretty complicated!

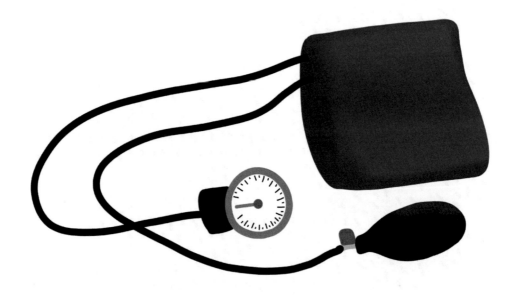

Someone will also put a wrap around your arm and blow it up like a balloon, then deflate it slowly while listening to your arm. Sounds pretty silly, right?

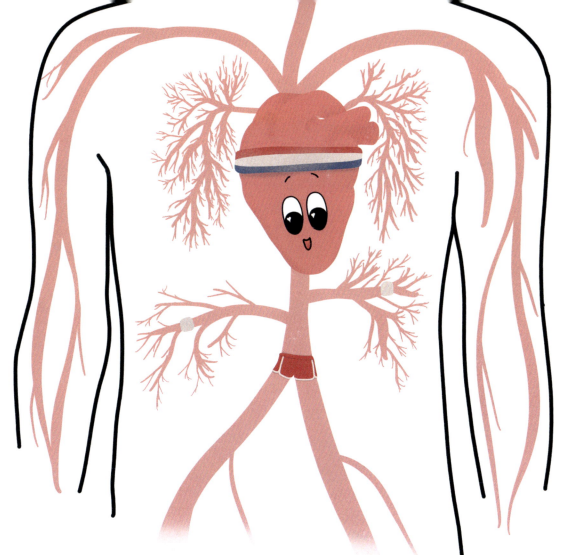

This is called a sphygmomanometer (whoa), or simply a blood pressure cuff. It helps measure how hard your heart is working to pump your blood.

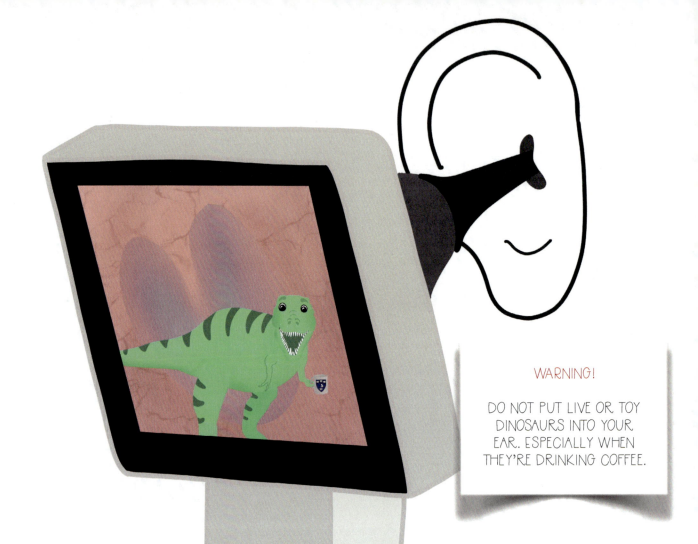

At some point, they will look into your ears, nose, and mouth to see if you have any infections or funny looking things in there.

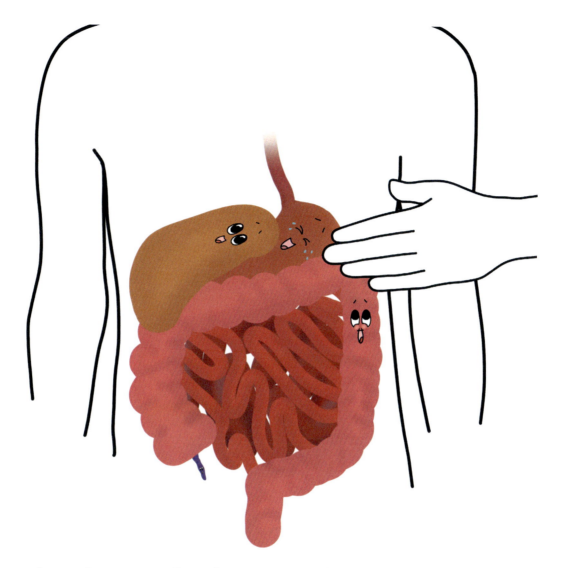

The doctor will also feel your belly to check all those ticklish organs. Those organs take nutrients from the food you eat and deliver them to your blood!

The doctor will also feel under your neck, near your armpits, and along other parts of your body for lymph nodes. Lymph nodes are part of your immune system and can swell if you are sick.

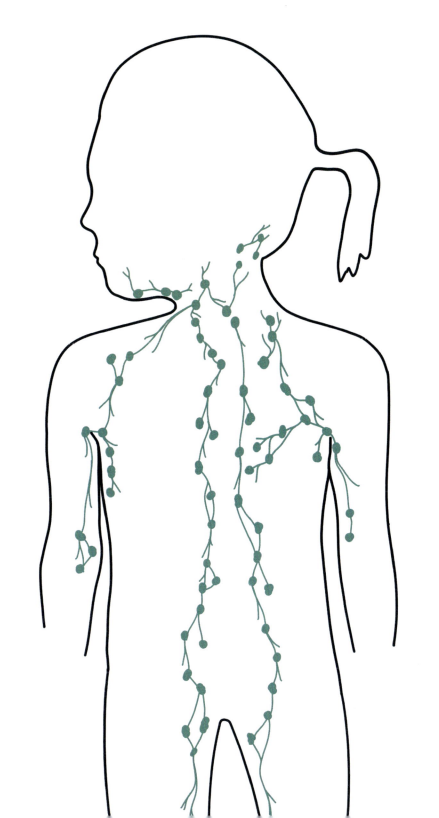

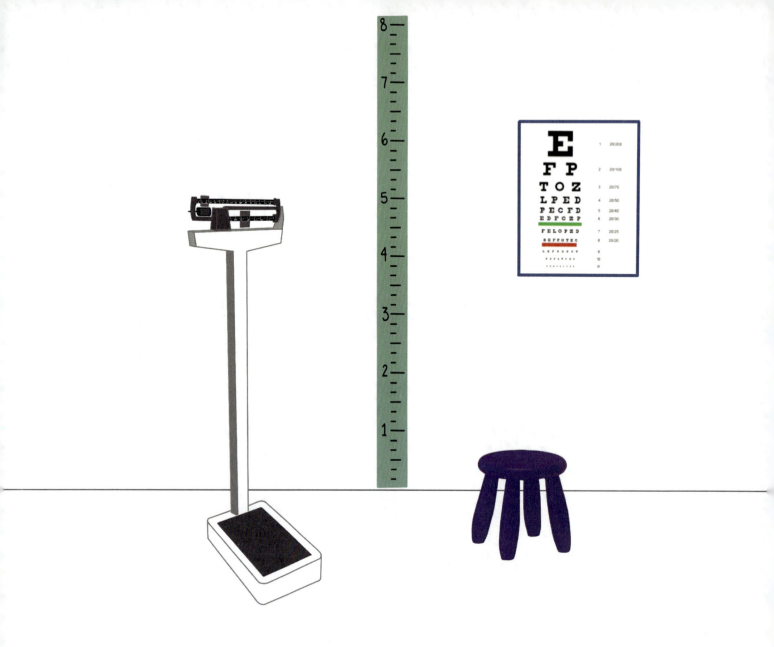

Someone will also check your eyes and measure your height and weight.

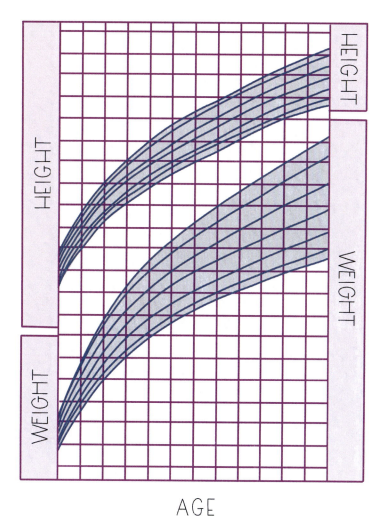

Healthy children can be many shapes and sizes, but they all tend to grow a certain amount each year. Doctors check to make sure you are growing the right amount.

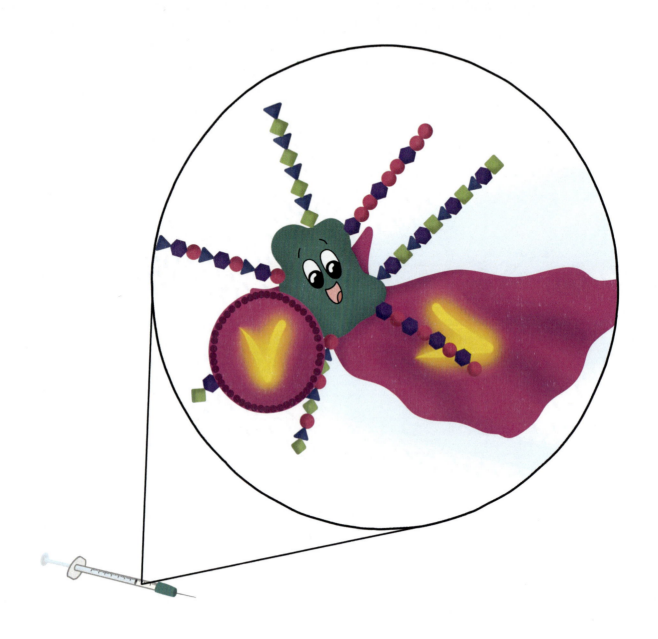

At the end of your checkup, you might get a vaccine. This is a way to stop some very bad germs from making you sick.

Most vaccines are shots, so it might hurt a little, but only for a second. Take a deep breath and know you are brave for keeping your body safe!

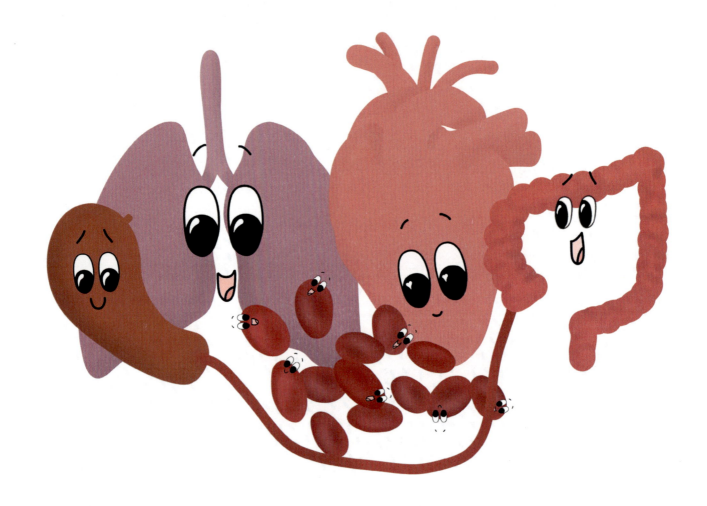

Going to the doctor's for a checkup can be a lot of fun! You can learn so much about your body and you should feel proud for taking such good care of it!

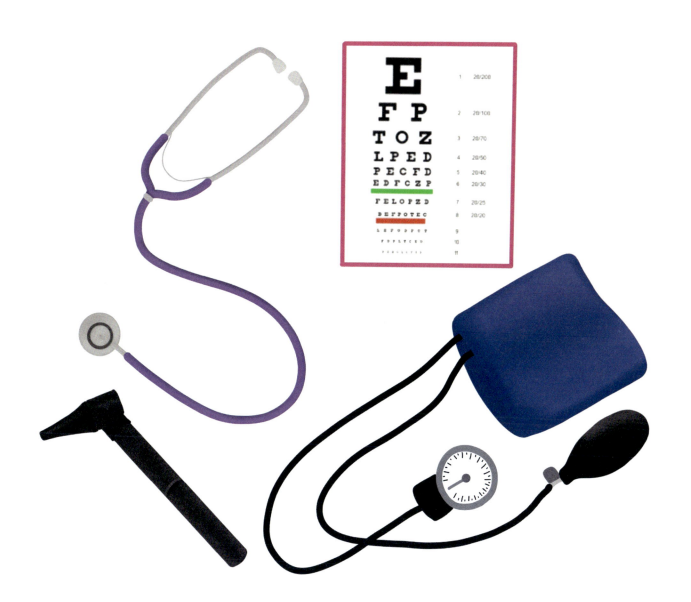

Maybe you can become a doctor one day!

Congratulations on completing

The Doctor's Visit : 101

Check out other books from:

Baby Medical School

And

The Baby Biochemist